Dedicated To:
My puppy, Ollie & all beloved pets

ritten By: Abigail Gartland

Hello, my name is St. Francis of Assisi!

I was born in 1181 in Assisi, Italy!

When I was a little boy, I had a very happy childhood, and I loved animals!

When I grew older, I made a mistake of going away from God.

During this time, I went to France and was very selfish.

I became a knight to fight in the war. I wanted to feel important and forgot about God.

After a while, I just realized that I wasn't very happy because I was serving myself and not God.

One day, as I rode my horse, I saw someone who was very sick and needed help.

I got off my horse, and kissed his hand. I didn't worry about getting sick.

He helped me realize that everyone is important and needs love.

During my prayers,
Jesus told me to
help everyone that I
could.

I followed Jesus' instructions and later started the Franciscan Friars.

I taught people to be kind to all. Kindness to animals is important, too!

Do you want to be more like me?

First, you can celebrate my feast day with me on October 4th!

October
4

Second, you can treat everyone and every animal with kindness!

Third, you can always listen to God in prayer!

I pray for you every day of your life.

St. Francis of Assisi, pray for us

About the Author

Abigail Gartland

love the saints and I love my faith. The
lea for sharing the stories of the saints
ith little ones came when my dear friends
ere expecting their first baby. I wanted to
eate something as unique and special as
ir friendship. Each book is dedicated to
ery special people and groups who have
iriched my faith in different ways. I am
essed to write these stories and
ppreciate the unending support of my
mily and friends. When I am not writing, I
n a middle school teacher. I hope you
ijoy these stories. I pray for each and
ery person who opens one of my books
 learn more about the saints.

Abbie